SPIRITED
COOKING

the intoxicating
delights of cooking with
spirits and liqueurs

SPIRITED
COOKING

consulting editor: Jenni Fleetwood

LORENZ BOOKS

This edition is published by Lorenz Books

Lorenz Books is an imprint of Anness Publishing Ltd
Hermes House, 88–89 Blackfriars Road, London SE1 8HA
tel. 020 7401 2077; fax 020 7633 9499
www.lorenzbooks.com; info@anness.com

© Anness Publishing Ltd 2003

UK agent: The Manning Partnership Ltd, 6 The Old Dairy,
Melcombe Road, Bath BA2 3LR; tel. 01225 478 444;
fax 01225 478 440; sales@manning-partnership.co.uk

UK distributor: Grantham Book Services Ltd, Isaac Newton Way,
Alma Park Industrial Estate, Grantham, Lincs NG31 9SD;
tel. 01476 541 080; fax 01476 541 061; orders@gbs.tbs-ltd.co.uk

North American agent/distributor: National Book Network,
4501 Forbes Boulevard, Suite 200, Lanham, MD 20706;
tel. 301 459 3366; fax 301 429 5746; www.nbnbooks.com

Australian agent/distributor: Pan Macmillan Australia, Level 18,
St Martins Tower, 31 Market St, Sydney, NSW 2000; tel. 1300 135 113;
fax 1300 135 103; customer.service@macmillan.com.au

New Zealand agent/distributor: David Bateman Ltd,
30 Tarndale Grove, Off Bush Road, Albany, Auckland;
tel. (09) 415 7664; fax (09) 415 8892

A CIP catalogue record for this book is available from the British
Library.

Publisher: Joanna Lorenz
Managing Editor: Helen Sudell
Senior Editor: Joanne Rippin
Original Text: Stuart Walton
Original Recipes: Norma Miller
Photographers: David Jordan and Janine Hosegood (cut outs)
Designer: Adelle Morris
Production controller: Darren Price

10 9 8 7 6 5 4 3 2 1

NOTES

Bracketed terms are intended for American readers.

For all recipes, quantities are given in both metric and imperial
measures and, where appropriate, measures are also given in
standard cups and spoons. Follow one set, but not a mixture,
because they are not interchangeable.

Standard spoon and cup measures are level.
1 tsp = 5ml, 1 tbsp = 15ml, 1 cup = 250ml/8fl oz

Australian standard tablespoons are 20ml. Australian readers should
use 3 tsp in place of 1 tbsp for measuring small quantities of gelatine,
flour, salt, etc.

Medium (US large) eggs are used unless otherwise stated.

CONTENTS

INTRODUCTION

Cooking with a drink at your elbow is a time-honoured tradition, and when the drink finds its way into the food, it adds a new and exciting dimension. This is especially true of spirits, liqueurs and fortified wines. Like essences, they have concentrated flavours. These may mirror other ingredients used, making it easy for the cook to decide which marriages will work – an orange liqueur with citrus fruit, for instance, or crème de fraise with strawberries.

The neutral drinks – such as gin, vodka and, to a lesser extent, ouzo – are ideal for enhancing existing flavours, adding a certain piquancy to sauces and soups. These spirits often work particularly well with fish and shellfish. They are also useful for adding to vegetable dishes, where the flavour is intended to flatter, rather than overwhelm the other ingredients.

Spirits, liqueurs and fortified wines all depend to some degree on distillation, either as an integral part of the manufacturing process or – in the case of fortified wines – by the addition of a distillate to ordinary table wine to make it stronger and perhaps sweeter.

Distillation is the extraction of higher alcohols from fermented drinks by heating them until the alcohol, which has a lower boiling point than water, vaporizes into steam. When the alcohol-laden steam hits a cool surface, it forms a dripping condensation, and reverts to a liquid with a higher concentration of alcohol than the original. If the process is repeated, the liquid will have even more alcohol by volume. Where a distilled drink

stops being a spirit and turns into a liqueur is a matter for debate. The one constant is that, to be a liqueur, a drink should have some obvious aromatizing element. This doesn't mean that all flavoured distillates are liqueurs – a flavoured vodka is still a vodka, but there are no neutral liqueurs.

Gradually, spirits, liqueurs and fortified wines have found their way into cookery, sometimes in dramatic fashion, as when cognac is ignited to give Crêpes Suzette a blazing brilliance. Certain dishes are constructed entirely around a particular drink; there would be no Crêpes Suzette without Cointreau, no Zabaglione without Marsala.

This book doesn't claim to be a comprehensive directory of every spirituous beverage ever invented; instead, it is a guide to those distilled drinks that can be used most successfully in cooking, whether they be spirits, liqueurs or fortified wines. You'll find advice in the introduction about labels to look out for. The liqueurs are grouped by flavour, so that if you lack the liqueur called for in a specific recipe, you can substitute something similar that will work just as well.

The recipes include classic favourites such as Sherry Trifle and Caribbean Rum Cake alongside spirited newcomers like Scallops with Pastis on Vegetable Rösti, and Chicken with Wild Mushrooms and Vermouth. Several of the items included would make delicious edible gifts. The only thing nicer than a beautifully wrapped bottle or a box of Mini Florentines, Bourbon Balls and Mocha Truffles would be a copy of this book, with a bottle of your friend's favourite tipple, of course.

A COOK'S GUIDE TO POPULAR SPIRITS AND LIQUEURS

There's an enormous variety of spirits, liqueurs and fortified wines. Just step into a good bottle store, or cast your eye over the selection in your favourite bar, and you may be surprised at the variety of shapes, sizes, colours and types available. What you use in the kitchen, however, will largely be determined by the contents of your own liquor cabinet, and how often you've been tempted to bring home alcoholic souvenirs from holidays abroad. In the pages that follow you'll find a guide to the most popular varieties, and some suggestions for using them in cooking. Liqueurs are grouped by flavour, so if you have purchased a mysterious bottle and haven't got a clue what to do with it, you should be able to discover which family it belongs to. Further information and practical advice is offered in the recipe section of this book.

ESSENTIAL SPIRITS

The art of distilling alcohol arose in Europe as a result of alchemical experiments designed to find the "elixir of life". The powerful brew that was arrived at by distilling was thought to contain the "soul" or "spirit" of the wine.

BRANDY

In the kitchen, brandy is very versatile, lending its delicious flavour to soups, pâtés, butters, robust meat dishes and delicate vegetable terrines. It goes well with both savoury and sweet dishes, and is popular for flaming.

COGNAC

The most famous of all brandies is cognac, named after a town in the Charente region of western France. Traders from the Netherlands went there in the 17th century principally to take delivery of consignments of salt, but also to stock up on the region's thin, acidic wine. Because of tax regulations, and to save space in the ships' holds, they boiled the wines to reduce their volume. The intention was to reconstitute them at the home port. However, when the traders returned to the Netherlands and uncorked the wine, they found it had benefited from the reduction process. From here it was a short step to distillation.

First produced in the early 18th century, Martell is a leading brand worldwide.

> ### TROU NORMANDE
>
> **In Normandy, there is a gastronomic tradition called** *trou normande*, **which literally means "Norman hole". A shot of neat Calvados is drunk in place of a sorbet (sherbet) before the main course of a meal. The idea is that the spirit punches a hole through the food that has already been eaten and makes room for more.**

Such was the fame and premium paid for the distilled wines of the Charente that there have been many imitations over the centuries. None, however, can replicate the precise local conditions in which cognac is made. The area's chalky soil, maritime climate and the ageing in Limousin oak barrels all contribute to making cognac the finest of all brandies.

The industry's first great entrepreneur was Jean Martell, a Jersey-born opportunist who, in 1715, gave up his career as a successful smuggler to found the house that still bears his name. Cognac's other leading brands are Hennessy, Courvoisier and Remy Martin. Smaller, but no less distinguished companies include Hine and Otard.

Cognac quality is classified by the length of time it has been aged. On the bottom rung for the British and Irish markets is VS (historically known as three-star and still identified by a row of stars on the label). VS may include brandies as young as three years old, but the basic products of most leading companies contain some significantly older reserves. The next stage up is

Courvoisier, Remy Martin and Hennessy brandies range from a youthful VS to a venerable XO.

VSOP (Very Special – or Superior – Old Pale). This fine cognac was originally designated five-star because the youngest spirit it contains must have spent at least five years in wood. At the upper end of the market is XO cognac – a venerable spirit with a price tag to match.

For cooking, it makes sense to use a relatively inexpensive cognac, but do not make the mistake of buying the cheapest bottle on the shelf. As when using wine in cooking, quality counts, and something that tastes rough in the glass will not do your food any favours.

ARMAGNAC

Armagnac is not quite as famous as cognac, but it has an even more illustrious pedigree, having been distilled in the Pays de Gascogne region of France since the 15th century. The wine that forms the basis of this type of brandy is derived from a blend of several grapes. The continuous still, invented by Edouard Adam, is widely used to distil Armagnac, and makers contend that it is thanks to the continuous distillation process that the spirit is so fragrant and full of character. The flavour tends to be quite dry, because it is not adjusted with colouring, and the absence of caramel (a permitted colouring used in some other types of brandy) makes Armagnac generally paler than a cognac of the same age. The labelling system is similar to that used for cognac, with VS, VSOP and XO denoting how long the brandy has been aged in the cask.

"Hors d'age" indicates long cask-aging.

FLAMING BRANDY

The easiest way to flambé a dish is to heat the spirit – usually brandy – in a metal soup ladle over medium heat. If you are heating it over a gas flame, it will probably ignite spontaneously; if using an electric hob, ignite the spirit using a long-handled match. Pour the burning spirit carefully over the food you wish to flambé, taking care not to burn yourself in the process.

BRANDIES FROM OTHER COUNTRIES

Outside France, Spain is the most significant producer of grape brandy. Top brands include Fundador, Lepanto, Cardinal Mendoza and Conde d'Osborne. From Greece comes Metaxa, a brandy that is marketed in three grades: three-star; five-star and seven-star. Metaxa tends to be slightly sweeter than cognac.

A leading Spanish brandy.

In the last thirty years or so, some fine aged spirits have been produced in the United States, capable of giving VSOP cognacs a run for their money. The insides of the oak casks are heavily charred, resulting in brandies of great richness and complexity. Look out for Germain-Robin and RMS.

Marc A by-product of wine production and the most celebrated is made in Burgundy (Marc de Bourgogne). It is said to aid digestion and is frequently served in France as an after-dinner drink. Grappa is an Italian version, and it is also produced in California.

Marc is a distillate of wine-making residue.

Calvados The most famous apple brandy, named after the region where it is made, spends a minimum of two years in the cask.

Applejack The American answer to Calvados, Laird's is one of the best-selling brands.

Like Calvados, Applejack is distilled from good quality cider.

WHISKY

One of the world's leading spirits, whisky has a history every bit as distinguished as that of cognac. Home distillation in Scotland, where the drink originated, can be traced back to the 15th century, when the practice of distilling surplus grain to make a potent drink for clan chieftains was established. Initially, the spirit was primarily valued for its medicinal powers, and early examples were no doubt infusions of herbs and berries rather than the pure grain product we know today.

The grain used can be barley, rye or corn, or a mixture of these. The most prized Scotch whiskies are made purely from barley. The grains are malted, which means that they are allowed to germinate in water before being lightly cooked. This encourages the formation of sugars, which in turn feed the yeast that produces the first ferment. A double distillation by the pot-still method results in a spirit that is then matured, often for decades, in oak barrels. When the whisky is produced exclusively at a single distillery, it is called a single malt. Vatted malts are the blended produce of several single malts.

Good whisky expresses its regional origins and the raw materials that go into it. Twenty-five-year-old malt will be shot through with all sorts of profoundly complex flavours and perfumes picked up from the wood in which it has matured and even – according to some pundits – the sea air that wafts around coastal distilleries.

Whiskies made from corn or unmalted barley are simply known as grain whiskies and are always considerably lighter in style than the malts. They could be called beginner's Scotch, as their principal use is in the production of blended Scotch – whisky made from a mixture of malt and grain products.

A rich peaty malt produced in Islay.

Scotch is naturally the only conceivable accompaniment for the ceremonial haggis on Burns Night (25 January). Un-iced Scotch also tastes great with hearty soups, such as Scotch broth or cock-a-leekie. Although the finest single malts are frequently drunk neat, it is widely believed that taming some of the spirit's fire helps to bring up the complicated array of flavours the drink contains. Scotch is therefore usually drunk with an equal quantity of water, ideally the same spring water that goes into the whisky itself.

IRISH WHISKEY

The origins of distillation in the Emerald Isle are at least as old as those of Scotch. Irish whiskey once enjoyed an unrivalled reputation as a more approachable style of spirit than Scotch malt. It was only when blended Scotch began to be made on a significant scale towards the end of the 19th century that Irish whiskey was nudged out of the frame.

The extra "e" in the spelling of the word whiskey is not the only thing that differentiates this spirit from Scotch. No peat is used in the kilns, so there is none of the smoky pungency that is present to some degree in most Scotch whisky. Also, Irish whiskey is inevitably a blend of malted and unmalted grain. There's a historical reason for this: punitive taxes on malted barley in the mid-19th century forced Irish distillers to produce a blended product long before this became common practice in Scotland. A third difference between Irish whiskey and Scotch concerns the distillation process. In Ireland, triple distillation by the copper pot-still

This whiskey is distilled at Middleton, near Cork.

method is used. The third distillation produces a product with a softer, ultra-refined palate profile, which still retains all of its complexity. By law, the spirit must be cask-aged for at least three years, though many Irish whiskeys are matured for considerably longer.

AMERICAN WHISKEY

The spelling is the same as Irish whiskey, but the grain used is different. Distillers in Bourbon County, Kentucky, experimented with pure corn whiskey and found a ready market for their product. Before long, Kentucky bourbon was well on its way to assuming a place in the ranks of the world's fine spirits.

Bourbon is a whiskey made from a mixture of not less than 50 per cent corn with malted barley, like a blended Scotch. The leading brand of bourbon is Jim Beam.

Tennessee Sour Mash Whiskey is different from bourbon, but equally distinctive. The newly made spirit is filtered through charcoal before being cask-matured, and the resulting whiskey is rich and smooth. The most famous brands are Jack Daniel's and Dickel.

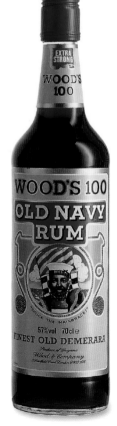

A bourbon whiskey from Kentucky.

OTHER WHISKY PRODUCING COUNTRIES

After Scotland, the United States and Ireland, Canada and Japan are major whisky producers. Canadian whiskies are blends of different grains, almost always containing some rye. The leading label is Hiram Walker's Canadian Club.

A rich and smooth Tennessee whiskey.

Japan has by far the youngest whisky industry. Among the more illustrious brands are Suntory's 12-year-old Pure Malt.

RUM

A spirit derived from distilling fermented molasses, rum is produced all over the West Indies and eastern South America, as well as in Mauritius, the Philippines, the USA and Australia. The flavour of the commercial white rums that lead the market is relatively neutral. Coloured rums are cask-aged, sometimes for decades, before being bottled.

Rum goes well with fruits, especially tropical fruits, and tastes delicious with banana, pineapple and coconut.

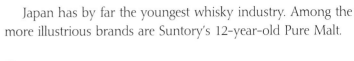

The golden Mount Gay rum has been aged for less time in the barrel than the Captain Morgan or Wood's Navy Rum.

GIN

One of the five essential spirits – along with brandy, whisky, rum and vodka – gin originated in 16th-century Holland. Like many other distilled drinks, it was originally intended to be medicinal. The juniper berries that are the principal flavouring – and the origin of the Dutch name, *genever* – are a diuretic, valuable for counteracting water retention.

It may well have been British soldiers returning home from the Thirty Years' War who first brought the taste for the Dutch grain spirit to Britain. The drink became hugely popular and in less than a hundred years, it was being distilled in London, using hops and barley, and was widely available and so cheap that it became excessively consumed by the poorest classes.

It was only in the late Victorian era that gin began to lose its dubious status as the corrosive solace of the destitute. Because of its colourlessness and absence of wood-derived richness, it began to be seen as a suitably ladylike alternative to Scotch whisky and cognac. New converts to the drink didn't wish to associate themselves with the negative image that gin had acquired, however, so resorted to euphemisms. For a while it was improbably referred to as "white wine".

The rehabilitation of gin continued with the invention of what was to become the world's favourite aperitif – gin and tonic – and today gin is once more immensely popular, but with a wider and more discriminatory public. In the kitchen, gin not only refreshes the cook, but is also a useful addition to fish and shellfish dishes. It tastes good with fruit such as apricots and peaches, and the juniper flavour means that it goes well with game.

Bombay Sapphire is more delicately aromatic than most other gins, and Gordon's is the brand leader among London gins.

VODKA

A potent spirit distilled from various grains – and occasionally potatoes – vodka is pure, unadulterated, uncomplicated alcohol. It has been made in Poland, Russia and the Baltic states of Latvia, Lithuania and Estonia since the early days of distillation in Europe.

Precisely when a drink recognizable as vodka emerged is debatable, but once home distillation had become a favoured way of passing long, grim northern winters, peasant families were producing their own vodkas on an extensive scale.

> ## SCHNAPPS
> **Of similar parentage to vodka, schnapps is a neutral grain and/or potato spirit, rectified to a high degree of purity. Fragrant spices supply the aroma. There are several fruit–flavoured versions, of which peach schnapps is perhaps the best known. Newcomers on the schnapps scene include butterscotch, chocolate and peppermint.**

KIRSCH

The original cherry spirit, kirsch is a colourless pure distillate. It is a true brandy or eau-de-vie, not to be confused with cherry brandy, which is a liqueur. A speciality of eastern France, it is also made in the Black Forest region of Bavaria, and is known as kirschwasser, and in Switzerland and Austria.

The cherries used are Morello, a type favoured for Black Forest Gateau. Use kirsch to add a richness to desserts, to soak the sponge base for a mousse or to moisten fresh fruit, such as pineapple. It goes well with apricots and almonds.

A cherry eau-de-vie with a unique identity.

The classic, smooth Stolichnaya Russian vodka, a vodka flavoured and coloured with chillies, and a delicious cherry version.

These early distillates would have tasted pretty rough. Herbs, seeds or berries were frequently steeped in the spirit to mask its rank flavour, unwittingly blazing the trail for the flavoured vodkas that would become popular centuries later.

Vodka will happily take up whatever flavouring producers choose to add, including lemon peel, bison grass, red chillies, cherries, rowan berries, saffron and liquorice. However, it is the neutral, ultra-purified grain vodka – made from wheat or rye – that has become so popular in the West, especially with younger drinkers.

Ice cold vodka is the classic accompaniment to fine caviar. In Scandinavian countries, it is also drunk with marinated and smoked fish, such as herring, mackerel and even salmon. It is famously mixed with tomato juice to make the drink known as a Bloody Mary, and the same combination can also be served as a stunning cold soup.

OUZO

Like anis and pastis, which it resembles, ouzo is made by steeping an aromatizing agent in a neutral, highly rectified alcohol base, usually of vegetable origin. As well as anise, spices such as cardamom, cinnamon, coriander and nutmeg are added, and exact recipes vary with the producers.

All these spirits turn milky when water is added. The predominantly anise flavour means that they go well with fish. In Greece, where ouzo originated, it is often cooked with squid, while in France, pastis and scallops form a winning combination. Vegetable dishes can be enhanced with a splash of these spirits. Pernod, a type of pastis often flavoured with liquorice, is a great accompaniment for spring vegetables, while anis tastes delicious in pumpkin soup.

A popular holiday tipple in sunny Greece.

LIQUEURS

Essentially a liqueur is any spirit-based drink to which flavouring elements have been added, usually by infusion, and – in the vast majority of cases – enhanced by sweetening.

HERBAL LIQUEURS

Among the most venerable and best-loved liqueurs are those that were developed by alchemists as medicinal drinks. Herbs such as hyssop or angelica were infused in alcohol to produce beverages that were claimed to cure all manner of ailments.

BÉNÉDICTINE

Said to contain as many as 75 herbs, spices and other aromatizing ingredients, this liqueur was developed in 1520 by a Benedictine monk in the monastery at Fécamp in the Normandy region of northern France. On tasting the bright golden elixir for the first time, the monk, Don Bernardo Vincelli, is said to have praised God for its excellence. The monastery continued to produce the cognac-based liqueur until the time of the French Revolution in 1789, when the monasteries were forcibly closed and production banned. It was revived some seventy years later, when Alexandre Le Grand discovered the secret recipe. So excited was he by the discovery that he built a new distillery at Fécamp so that the drink could be

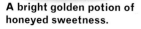

A bright golden potion of honeyed sweetness.

The yellow Chartreuse is sweeter and of normal spirit strength, while the green is intensely powerful and aromatic.

revived. It was Le Grand who gave the liqueur the name Bénédictine, in honour of its heritage, and it has flourished ever since. It is a popular ingredient in desserts.

CHARTREUSE

Unlike Bénédictine, Chartreuse is still made by monks – of the Carthusian order. Their monastery is close to the distillery at Voiron, near Grenoble. The recipe is a secret one, known only to three people at any one time, but is believed to contain more than 130 herbs and plants. The original liqueur – labelled as "elixir végétal de la Grande-Chartreuse" is extremely potent. More freely available are yellow Chartreuse, a punchy greenish-yellow liqueur that is sweet, honeyed and slightly minty in flavour, and green Chartreuse, a somewhat less alcoholic concoction, which is pale green and has a less pungent herbal aroma. In France, green Chartreuse is sometimes added to hot chocolate, while the yellow version is used to fortify coffee. The liqueur also works well in a savoury context, especially with seafood.

DRAMBUIE

Hugely popular the world over, especially in the United States, Drambuie is Scotland's contribution to the world's classic liqueurs. A unique combination of fine malt and straight grain whisky, heather honey and herbs, the recipe is said to have been given as a reward to one Captain Mackinnon in 1745, after the defeat at Culloden by Bonnie

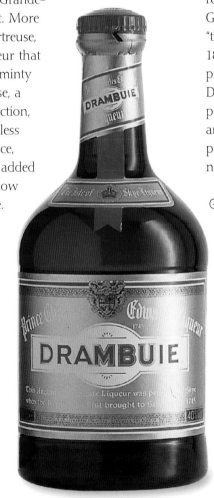

Scotland's contribution to the world's classic liqueurs.

Prince Charlie. It's a tale much polished in the telling, but the truth is probably more prosaic. Historians now believe that the drink was a typical blend of the period, made by the Mackinnons and given to the fugitive prince to revive his spirits when he arrived in Skye on the first leg of his journey to France. Either way, it is still produced by the Mackinnon family. They registered the name (from the Gaelic *an dram buidheach*, "the drink that satisfies") in 1892. It has been in commercial production since 1906. Drambuie tastes wonderful poured over rich Dundee cake, and is also a great addition to a pecan pie filling. For a savoury note, try it with venison steaks.

The original formula for Glayva is a great deal older than the liqueur itself.

GLAYVA

Like Drambuie, Glayva is a Scotch whisky-based liqueur, but it is of much more recent provenance. The drink was first formulated just after the Second World War. Its aromatizers are quite similar to those of Drambuie, although its flavour is intriguingly different. Heather honey and various herbs are used, and so is a quantity of orange peel, resulting in a far fruitier attack on the palate.

The noble Scot commemorated in the case of Glayva is Master Borthwick, the 16-year-old credited with carrying Robert the Bruce's heart back to Scotland after the King's defeat at the hands of the Saracens. The indomitable lad cut off the head of a Saracen chieftain and brought that back too, just to keep his spirits up. All of those public houses named the Saracen's Head recall the event.

Like other Scotch-based liqueurs, Glayva is particularly good added to ice cream.

Citrus-flavoured Liqueurs

Oranges and tangerines are the fruits most frequently used, with brandy as the favoured spirit. All citrus-flavoured liqueurs work wonderfully well drizzled over ice cream.

GRAND MARNIER

The best-loved of all the orange-flavoured liqueurs, Grand Marnier was the invention of Louis-Alexandre Marnier. On a visit to Haiti he encountered bitter oranges, and hit upon the idea of blending their juice with top-quality cognac. Several other orange-flavoured liqueurs are made in a similar way, but Grand Marnier differs in that the blend is then re-distilled, sweetened and aged in the cask. The result is a highly refined, mellow full-strength spirit with a warm amber colour and an intense, festive scent of ripe oranges. Grand Marnier is sweet, but the cognac on which it is based prevents it from being cloying when served straight. It is the classic ingredient in duck à l'orange and is used in a wide range of desserts and sweetmeats, including ice cream and flamed crêpes.

Grand Marnier is a little younger than its big French rival Cointreau, and the style of it is quite different.

CURAÇAO

Originally, Curaçao was made on the Caribbean island of the same name, close to the coast of Venezuela. A popular variant name for this orange liqueur is Triple Sec. To counter the sweetness of Curaçao, some cooks (and cocktail bartenders) like to add a few drops of orange bitters.

Curaçao can be a range of colours, but all are flavoured with oranges.

COINTREAU

A double distillation of grape brandy infused with orange peel, Cointreau is fundamentally a version of Curaçao. It was originally sold as Triple Sec White Curaçao, but when many other proprietary Curaçaos began to be sold as Triple Sec the Cointreau brothers who made the liqueur decided to give it their family name. Produced in the Loire Valley in France, and also in the Americas, Cointreau is very popular. Despite its spirit strength, it tastes relatively innocuous. It is sugar-sweet and colourless, but has a powerful fume of fresh oranges, with hints of the herbs that are part of the secret recipe. The oranges used in Cointreau are a blend of bitter green Seville-style varieties from the Caribbean and a sweeter type from the south of France. The liqueur tastes good in orange sauces to accompany duck or game, and is delicious in chocolate mousse.

MANDARINE NAPOLÉON

A vivid yellow-orange liqueur, Mandarine Napoléon is made from the skins of Sicilian tangerines, which are steeped in cognac and other French brandies. The spirit is then distilled again, sweetened, coloured with carotene and matured for several months.

The drink has a colourful history. When the tangerine first arrived in Europe at the end of the 18th century, there was quite a craze for it. In recognition of its Chinese origins, the French named the fruit *mandarine.* Steeping the peel in cognac after eating the fruit became a popular pastime, one that the Emperor Napoleon Bonaparte himself enjoyed. He introduced the resulting drink to his friend, the chemist Antoine-François de Fourcroy, who jotted down the recipe. Years later, the recipe came into the hands of the Belgian distiller, Louis Schmidt, who made the liqueur and named it after the emperor.

The drink is a highly individual product that has since won several international awards. Every year, the makers of Mandarine Napoléon host competitions, where chefs from all over France prepare regional

A French invention now produced in Belgium.

South Africa's answer to Curaçao.

Cointreau is a double distillation of grape brandy, infused with orange peel and other secret plant ingredients.

dishes featuring the liqueur. Mandarine Napoléon goes well with poached mandarins and in orange-flavoured ice creams and mousses, but also works well in stuffings and sauces for duck, game and even seafood.

OTHER CITRUS LIQUEURS

Cuaranta Y Tres The Spanish name of this liqueur translates as "43", which is the number of ingredients it contains. Vanilla and citrus are the dominant flavours. It is also marketed as Licor 43.

Limoncello Made from whole lemons that are steeped for months in neutral alcohol, this has a sharp, almost sherbet flavour that sizzles on the tongue. Also sold as Lemonello, it is delicious chilled with soda water, and makes a good addition to a lemon sorbet (sherbet). Don't use too much, or it will inhibit the freezing process.

Tuaca This Italian favourite is brandy-based. It is flavoured with vanilla, citrus fruits and caramel, and is good for cooking as well as drinking either hot mixed with cappuccino, or cold poured over ice.

Van der Hum This South African liqueur is based on Cape brandy, flavoured with the peels of a type of tangerine known locally as "naartjies". Herbs and spices, especially nutmeg, are often added.

Coffee liqueur, when added to icy milk, makes a delicious long drink.

COFFEE LIQUEURS

Sweet, satisfying liqueurs have long been seen as the perfect foil for strong black coffee, and from there it was but a short step to adding the coffee flavour into the liqueurs themselves.

KAHLÚA

The label on the round-shouldered bottle shows a somnolent figure, sombrero tilted over his eyes as he leans against a wall on the outskirts of a Mexican town. The liqueur is Kahlúa, a dark brown coffee-flavoured essence that was very popular with younger drinkers in the eighties, when it was often mixed with vanilla ice cream to make the boozy dessert known as Dom Pedro. Although conceived in Mexico, and still produced in that country using locally-grown coffee beans, it is also made under licence in Europe. Kahlúa tastes good served chilled. Pour it over crushed ice in a tall glass, and float some thick cream on top. The liqueur also works well in coffee and chocolate desserts and cakes, and goes well with almonds and macadamia nuts. It is thought to give a smoother result than the more commonly used Tia Maria.

TIA MARIA

Deep brown and velvety, Tia Maria comes from Jamaica. It is based on dark rum and is flavoured with Blue Mountain coffee beans and local spices. Although the liqueur is sweet, sweeter than Kahlúa, for example, the aromatic components prevent it from being cloying. It is wonderful for lacing chocolate desserts and makes a good liqueur coffee, especially when the hot drink is made from the same Blue Mountain coffee beans.

BAILEY'S IRISH CREAM

A blend of Irish whiskey and cream, flavoured with coffee, Bailey's became chic in the 1970s, but was saddled with the image of the kind of drink with which unscrupulous boys plied unsuspecting girls in nightclubs. Since then, however, the popularity of cream liqueurs has grown, and Bailey's is still very much on the scene. Its sweet, creamy flavour makes it a good choice for adding to desserts, and it is particularly good in a coffee bavarois or an old-fashioned coffee cream.

All these liqueurs benefit from being served poured over ice, are delicious with coffee and can be used to enhance various desserts.

FRUIT AND NUT LIQUEURS

For the cook, fruit and nut liqueurs are an invitation to experimentation. Echo the flavour of the main ingredient by using the appropriate liqueur – crème de framboise with raspberries, for instance – or create an exciting mix by adding a nut liqueur like amaretto to chocolate or coffee.

CRÈME DE FRAMBOISE

Although the name suggests a cream liqueur, the "crème" indicates that it is sweet, as distinct from a dry spirit such as cognac or Calvados. Crème liqueurs generally consist of a neutral-tasting grape brandy with a flavouring. Usually a fruit or herb, the flavouring is either infused or macerated in the spirit, rather than being distilled. Typical examples are crème de banane (banana); cassis (blackcurrant); fraise (strawberry) and menthe (mint). Crème de cacao is based on chocolate. The deep red colour of crème de framboise reflects its raspberry flavouring. It is delicious poured over the berry fruit, which can then be served with meringues and cream.

MARASCHINO

A clear liqueur derived from an infusion of pressed Marasca cherry skins in a cherry-stone distillate, it is sweetened with sugar syrup and aged for several years before going on the market. Unlike the crème fruit liqueurs, it remains colourless. It should have a pronounced bitter cherry aroma, backed up by the nuttiness of the cherry stones. The best grades of maraschino are smooth enough to drink on their own, but sweeter brands are better chilled. In the kitchen, maraschino is an incomparable ingredient for soaking sponge for a layered cake. It tastes wonderful over fresh cherries, but is also good with other fruits, including peaches and apricots.

AMARETTO

Of all the liqueurs that rely on almonds for the principal flavouring, amaretto is the most famous. Made by steeping almond extracts, apricot kernels and seeds in brandy, this sweet, deep brown liqueur tastes like liquid marzipan.

These liqueurs offer a variety of fruit and nut flavours to add to other ingredients to make delicious combinations.

The flavour of the most popular brand, Disaronno Amaretto, is complex enough to be enjoyed on its own, but it works better chilled. Serve it frappe (over crushed ice).

In the kitchen, try it in a syrup for fruit salad, especially one that includes apricots. It tastes great poured over ratafia biscuits (almond macaroons) in a trifle, but maybe its best contribution is as the main flavouring in a superb ice cream.

FRANGELICO

A delicate straw-coloured liqueur flavoured with hazelnuts and herbs, Frangelico is delicious and not too sweet. It works well with nut desserts and cakes, especially those based on hazelnuts, and also complements the flavour of coffee or chocolate: try whipping it into softened coffee or chocolate ice cream. Like other nut liqueurs, it goes well with rich, dark fruit cake. Served chilled, a glass of Frangelico makes a surprisingly successful accompaniment to a piece of mature Stilton.

The bottle is designed to resemble a monk.

FORTIFIED WINES

Traditional fortified wines like port, sherry and Madeira have long held a favoured place in the kitchen, their intense flavours giving depth to sweet and savoury dishes. Vermouth, aromatized with herbs, tastes good with fish and shellfish.

PORT

The only major fortified wine to be based on red wine, port comes from the Douro valley, northern Portugal. It originated in the 17th century, when a punitive tax levy imposed on French goods by the English forced many wine shippers to source red wine in Portugal. As was the practice then, they fortified the wine with a little brandy for the voyage. This fortified drink, which soon became known as port, was dry, since the wine it contained was fermented. However, the chance discovery of the effects of fortification on an extremely ripe, sweet wine then led to port being remodelled. The normal fermentation was interrupted or "muted" with brandy or grape spirit to preserve sweetness.

Port is aged in the cask for various periods to produce different grades. Vintage ports are wines of a single year. Intended for long ageing, they must be bottled within two years of harvest. Late-bottled vintage (LBV) is also the product of a single year, but is kept in the cask for about six years before being bottled.

Port is excellent with nuts and mature, strong hard cheeses. It tastes better with Cheddar than with its traditional partner, Stilton. Its robust flavour makes it a good choice for cooking with rabbit or venison.

An LBV from a small Portuguese producer.

The production process for sherry is one of the most complicated for any fortified wine. Muy seco is the driest sherry.

SHERRY

Fortified wines bearing the name sherry have been produced around the world for well over a century, but true sherry comes only from a demarcated region in the southern Spanish province of Andalucia. The three main areas of production are Jerez de la Frontera; Puerto de Santa Maria and Sanlucar de Barrameda. Other countries that produce sherry-style wines are Australia, the United States, South Africa and Cyprus.

If you are using sherry in a savoury dish, such as the batter for a vegetable tempura, choose a dry variety. Dry sherry is delicious in a sauce for a fish dish and also makes a good addition to a pork stew. For desserts, like the classic sherry trifle, choose a sweeter variety, but don't opt for something cheap and nasty. Using a good quality sherry will add depth to the dish, but a sickly sweet and somewhat synthetic-tasting sherry will spoil it.

Madeiras range from sweet, rich Malmsey, to the only slightly sweet Verdelho and the palest and driest of all, Sercial.

MADEIRA

From the island of the same name, Madeira is made from a light, white base wine, sometimes supplemented with juice from local red grapes, *tinta negra mole*. For the sweeter styles, Bual and Malmsey, fermentation may be interrupted early by the addition of grape spirit, so that they retain natural sugar. The drier wines – Sercial and Verdelho – are fermented until more sugar has been consumed before they are fortified. The wines are then aged in the cask, during which time they are heated, either by the system known as an *estufa* ("stove"), or by being left in the hottest part of the winery or "lodge"– the wine may be labelled *vinho canteiro*. Madeiras are graded by the length of aging: Reserve is roughly five years old; Special Reserve is aged for about 10 years and Extra Reserve about 15 years. Dry Madeiras such as Sercial are good in consommé, while sweeter ones work well in fruit cakes and desserts.

MARSALA

Even more popular in the kitchen than Madeira, Marsala is a vital ingredient in desserts such as zabaglione and tiramisù. It is also used in a savoury context, to enhance the rich sauce traditionally served with veal scaloppini. All these dishes are Italian in origin, which is only fitting for a drink that comes from Sicily. Marsala is made from light white wines, which are fortified with grape spirit or sweetened and strengthened with alcohol-boosted juice from ultra-sweet late harvest grapes.

VERMOUTH

The distinctive character of vermouth owes much to the aromatizing herbs and botanical ingredients that are used to flavour it before bottling. Vermouth is based on low-alcohol, mostly white wine, which may be allowed a short period of ageing before being fortified with spirits. For the sweeter versions, sugar syrup may be added. After absorption of the flavourings – a process that is encouraged by stirring the mixture with wooden paddles – the vermouth is bottled at around 17 per cent ABV (alcohol by volume). Brands vary according to the number of herbal ingredients added, and ingredients include cloves, cinnamon, quinine, citrus peel and ginger. Vermouth can be red or white, dry or sweet. Martini Extra Dry is the leading brand worldwide. Another bone-dry pale vermouth is the French Noilly Prat. Cinzano Bianco is a popular sweet, white vermouth, while reds include Italian Munt e Mes, which combines sweet and bitter elements. Quinine gives Dubonnet its appetizing bitterness.

The herbal ingredients in dry vermouth add a savoury note to fish, chicken and mushroom dishes. Vermouth sauce tastes good with herb–stuffed lemon sole.

Very dry vermouth from the south of France.

COOKING WITH SPIRITS AND LIQUEURS

Spirits, liqueurs and fortified wines have a definite role to play in the kitchen. Their strength of flavour means that even relatively small amounts make a huge difference to dishes, rounding the flavour of sauces and stews and giving desserts a luxurious richness. Whether you are taking the edge off summer's heat by indulging in a bowl of iced Tomato and Vodka Soup, or spooning up a sweet treat in the shape of a Soufflé with Grand Marnier Ice Cream, there's every reason for raiding the liquor cabinet on a regular basis.

Having a tiny tot in the kitchen isn't always a good idea, but when the tot is one of brandy or whisky, and is being used to create an utterly delicious dish, there's no better way of getting into the party spirit.

PUMPKIN SOUP WITH ANIS

The flavour of anis goes remarkably well with pumpkin, softening the sweetness and giving an exciting new dimension to an everyday winter soup.

SERVES 4

675g/1½ lb pumpkin

30ml/2 tbsp olive oil

2 large onions, sliced

1 garlic clove, crushed

2 fresh red chillies, seeded and chopped

5ml/1 tsp curry paste

750ml/1¼ pints/3 cups vegetable or chicken stock

15ml/1 tbsp anis

150ml/¼ pint/⅔ cup single (light) cream

salt and ground black pepper

1 Peel the pumpkin, remove the seeds and chop the flesh into cubes.

2 Heat the oil and fry the onion slices until golden. Stir in the garlic, chillies and curry paste. Cook for 1 minute, then add the chopped pumpkin and cook for 5 minutes more, stirring occasionally, to coat the pumpkin in the spicy mixture.

3 Pour over the stock and season with salt and pepper. Bring to the boil, reduce the heat, cover and simmer for 25 minutes, or until the pumpkin is very soft.

4 Process until smooth in a blender or food processor, then return to the clean pan. Stir in the anis and reheat gently. Taste, and adjust the seasoning if necessary. Serve the soup in individual heated bowls, adding a generous spoonful of cream to each portion.

VARIATION

Pernod or ouzo could be used instead of anis. Adjust the quantity according to taste. The effect should be subtle rather than strident.

ICED TOMATO and VODKA SOUP

This fresh-flavoured soup packs a punch like a frozen Bloody Mary. It is the perfect soup for a hot day and makes a great prelude to a barbecue meal.

SERVES 4

450g/1lb ripe, well-flavoured tomatoes, roughly chopped

600ml/1 pint/2½ cups jellied beef stock or consommé

1 small red onion, quartered or roughly chopped

2 celery sticks, cut into large pieces

1 garlic clove

15ml/1 tbsp tomato purée (paste)

10ml/2 tsp lemon juice

10ml/2 tsp Worcestershire sauce

handful of small fresh basil leaves

30ml/2 tbsp vodka

salt and ground black pepper

crushed ice, 4 small celery sticks and sun-dried tomato bread, to serve

COOK'S TIP

The celery sticks are used to stir the soup and make edible dippers. They taste delicious this way, so have some extras in a pitcher or bowl of iced water on the table. Tall, thin glass vases are great for displaying celery sticks. Remove any tired or misshapen leaves, but leave the rest on.

1 Put the tomatoes, jellied stock or consommé, onion, celery, garlic and tomato purée in a blender or food processor and process until completely smooth.

2 Press the mixture through a sieve into a large bowl. Stir in the lemon juice, Worcestershire sauce, basil leaves and vodka.

3 Add salt and pepper to taste. Cover and chill in the refrigerator for at least 4 hours, preferably overnight.

4 Spoon a little crushed ice into four soup bowls and divide the soup among them. Place a celery stick in each bowl. Serve with chunks of toasted sun-dried tomato bread.

BOURBON PANCAKES with ASPARAGUS and PROSCIUTTO

A little bourbon in the batter makes for delicious Scotch pancakes. The same flavour is used
in the delectable dressing for the asparagus and prosciutto.

SERVES 4

50g/2oz/½ cup self-raising
(self-rising) flour

2.5ml/½ tsp mustard powder

1 egg, beaten

60ml/4 tbsp milk

15ml/1 tbsp bourbon

8 cooked asparagus spears

8 slices prosciutto

for the dressing

45ml/3 tbsp olive oil

15ml/1 tbsp bourbon

salt and ground black pepper

COOK'S TIPS
• If the batter is at all lumpy,
press it through a strainer into
a clean bowl or pitcher.
• An electric frying pan is great
for making the pancakes, since
the temperature can be
controlled. The surface area will
probably be larger, too, and
you may be able to cook all the
pancakes at the same time.

1 Sift the flour and mustard powder into a bowl. Make a well in the centre and add the beaten egg, milk and bourbon. Whisk the liquids, gradually incorporating the surrounding dry ingredients to make a smooth batter.

2 Heat a griddle or a heavy frying pan. Grease the surface thoroughly. Drop spoonfuls of the batter, making sure they are well spaced, on to the hot griddle to make four Scotch pancakes. For evenly shaped pancakes pour the batter into greased baking rings. Cook for 2–3 minutes until bubbles rise to the surface of each pancake and burst.

3 Using a slim spatula or palette knife, turn the pancakes over. Cook for 2–3 minutes more, until golden brown. Remove and keep hot while making four more pancakes in the same way.

4 Make the dressing by mixing the oil and bourbon in a bowl. Whisk well, then add salt and pepper to taste.

5 Place two pancakes on each plate. Put an asparagus spear on top of each pancake, drape decoratively with a slice of prosciutto and spoon over a little of the dressing. Serve at once.

STEP 1

VEGETABLE TEMPURA WITH SHERRY DIPPING SAUCE

A selection of vegetables, coated in a light batter and deep-fried, makes a marvellous starter. This traditional Japanese dish is served with a fiery mustard-like paste, grated mooli and a dipping sauce.

SERVES 4

1 red (bell) pepper, seeded and cut into diamond shapes

2 courgettes (zucchini), sliced

2 carrots, cut into batons

1 small mooli (daikon), sliced

handful of celery leaves

wasabi paste and grated mooli (daikon) with carrot shapes and celery leaves, to serve

for the batter

300ml/½ pint/1¼ cups water

1 egg, lightly beaten

115g/4oz/1 cup plain (all-purpose) flour

oil, for frying

for the dipping sauce

150ml/¼ pint/⅔ cup dashi (Japanese stock) or vegetable stock

75ml/5 tbsp soy sauce

60ml/4 tbsp dry sherry

30ml/2 tbsp caster (superfine) sugar

1 Pat the prepared vegetables with kitchen paper to ensure that they are completely dry. Make the dipping sauce by mixing all the ingredients in a bowl. Stir until the sugar has dissolved. Pour into individual bowls.

2 Make the batter by mixing the water and egg in a bowl. Sprinkle over the flour and stir until just mixed; the batter should be lumpy.

3 Heat the oil until a little batter added to it sinks and then quickly rises again. Dip the vegetables in the batter and fry a few at a time in the hot oil. As soon as they are golden all over, remove and drain on kitchen paper. Keep hot while you cook the rest.

4 Serve the tempura with the dipping sauce and wasabi. Offer a bowl of grated mooli, garnished with shaped carrot slices and celery leaves, as a palate cleanser.

COOK'S TIPS
• Dashi is a Japanese stock made from seaweed. Instant dashi is available from Asian stores.
• Mooli (daikon) is a variety of white radish.

STEP 3

SCALLOPS WITH PASTIS ON VEGETABLE RÖSTI

The combination of crisp vegetable cakes and sweet, tender scallops is superb. The flavour provided by the pastis echoes the taste of the dill that is used in the sauce and as a garnish for this excellent first course.

SERVES 4

30ml/2 tbsp sunflower oil

2 shallots, chopped

1 green (bell) pepper, seeded and chopped

8 large scallops, halved

3 fresh dill sprigs, chopped

15ml/1 tbsp pastis

150ml/¼ pint/⅔ cup fish or chicken stock

2.5ml/½ tsp lemon juice

salt and ground black pepper

fresh dill sprigs, to garnish

for the rosti

2 carrots

1 large courgette (zucchini)

1 parsnip

1 small potato

1 egg, lightly beaten

oil, for frying

1 Make the rösti. Coarsely grate the carrots, courgette, parsnip and potato into a bowl. Add the egg and stir to bind the mixture.

2 Heat a little oil in a large frying pan. Drop 3–4 heaped spoonfuls of the vegetable mixture into the oil. Flatten slightly with the back of a metal spoon, then cook for 8–10 minutes, or until golden, turning once. Remove from the pan and keep hot while cooking more rösti.

3 Heat the sunflower oil in a separate frying pan and fry the shallots and green pepper for 6–8 minutes. Add the scallops, chopped dill, pastis, stock and lemon juice and poach for 2 minutes. Season to taste. Spoon the mixture on to the vegetable rösti, garnish with dill and serve.

STEP 3

SALMON CEVICHE WITH GIN AND LIME

Marinating the salmon in a mixture of gin and lime juice "cooks" the fresh fish and gives it a marvellous flavour. For a tasty alternative, marinate strips of very fresh sea bass, bream, halibut or cod.

SERVES 4

675g/1½lb salmon fillet, skinned

1 small red onion, thinly sliced

6 fresh chives

6 fennel sprigs

3 fresh parsley sprigs

2 limes

30ml/2 tbsp gin

45ml/3 tbsp olive oil

sea salt and ground black pepper

extra chives and salad leaves, to serve

1 Cut the salmon fillet into very thin slices, taking care to remove any remaining bones with tweezers. Lay the pieces in a wide, shallow glass or pottery dish. Scatter the onion slices, chives, fennel and parsley sprigs over the salmon pieces.

2 Remove a few fine strips of rind from one of the limes and put them to one side for the garnish. Cut off the remaining rind, avoiding the pith, and slice it roughly. Squeeze the lime juice into a pitcher and add the sliced rind, along with the gin and olive oil. Whisk in sea salt and pepper to taste. Pour the dressing over the fish and mix gently.

3 Cover the dish with clear film (plastic wrap) and chill in the refrigerator for 4 hours, stirring occasionally. To serve, transfer to a platter. Scatter over the reserved strips of lime rind and add the extra chives, and salad leaves.

COOK'S TIP
Make this dish on the day you intend to serve it.

STEP 1

PAN-FRIED SQUID WITH OUZO

This delicious seafood dish takes very little time to make, so is ideal for an easy meal after a visit to the movies or theatre. Ouzo and lemon juice add a piquant note.

SERVES 4

500g/1¼lb prepared squid

30ml/2 tbsp olive oil

30ml/2 tbsp sesame seeds

15ml/1 tbsp green peppercorns

2 garlic cloves, crushed

6 spring onions (scallions), sliced

25g/1oz drained canned anchovies, chopped

tender bulb portion of 1 lemon grass stalk, sliced

15ml/1 tbsp chopped fresh parsley

15ml/1 tbsp torn fresh basil leaves

150ml/¼ pint/⅔ cup fish stock

10ml/2 tsp lemon juice

10ml/2 tsp ouzo

75g/3oz/¾ cup mangetouts (snow peas)

salt

fresh basil sprigs and pieces of cooked poppadom, to garnish

1 Cut the squid into strips, rinse under cold water, drain and pat dry with kitchen paper.

2 Heat the oil in a frying pan or wok and toast the sesame seeds with the green peppercorns for a few seconds.

3 Add the garlic, spring onions and squid. Toss to coat in the sesame mixture.

4 Stir in the anchovies, lemon grass, chopped parsley and basil. Pour in the stock, lemon juice and ouzo and simmer for about 12 minutes.

5 Add the mangetouts and cook for 2 minutes more. Season with salt and serve on individual plates. Garnish with basil and pieces of poppadom. Serve immediately.

COOK'S TIP
Some canned anchovies are extremely salty. To moderate the flavour, soak them in cold milk for 30 minutes. Drain and chop before using.

STEP 3

1.5kg/3-3½lb red snapper, cleaned

30ml/2 tbsp sunflower oil

1 onion, chopped

2 garlic cloves, crushed

50g/2oz/¾ cup button (white) mushrooms, sliced

5ml/1 tsp ground coriander

15ml/1 tbsp chopped fresh parsley

30ml/2 tbsp grated fresh root ginger

2 fresh red chillies, seeded and sliced

15ml/1 tbsp cornflour (cornstarch)

45ml/3 tbsp gin

300ml/½ pint/1¼ cups chicken or vegetable stock

salt and ground black pepper

for the garnish

15ml/1 tbsp sunflower oil

6 garlic cloves, sliced

1 lettuce heart, finely shredded

1 bunch fresh coriander (cilantro), tied with red raffia (optional)

STEP 3

RED SNAPPER WITH CHILLI, GIN AND GINGER SAUCE

A whole baked fish always looks impressive, and when a red snapper is stuffed with a tasty mushroom and garlic mixture and topped with ginger and chillies, it acquires a wonderful flavour. Gin transforms the cooking juices into a superb sauce.

1 Preheat the oven to 190°C/375°F/Gas 5. Grease a flameproof dish large enough to hold the fish. Make several diagonal cuts on one side of the fish.

2 Heat the oil in a frying pan and fry the onion, garlic and mushrooms for 2–3 minutes. Stir in the ground coriander and chopped parsley. Season with salt and pepper.

3 Stuff the cavity of the fish with the mushroom mixture, then carefully lift the fish into the dish. Pour in enough cold water to cover the bottom of the dish. Sprinkle the ginger and chillies over, then cover with foil and bake for 30–40 minutes, basting the fish occasionally. Remove the foil for the last 10 minutes.

4 Carefully lift the snapper on to a serving dish and keep hot. Tip the cooking juices into a pan.

5 Mix the cornflour and gin in a cup and stir into the cooking juices. Pour in the stock. Bring to the boil, reduce the heat and simmer for 3–4 minutes, stirring all the time until the sauce thickens. Taste for seasoning, then pour into a sauce-boat and keep hot.

6 Make the garnish. Heat the oil in a small pan and stir-fry the sliced garlic and shredded lettuce over a high heat until crisp. Spoon the garnish alongside the snapper. If using the coriander bouquet, place it on the other side. Serve with the sauce.

FISH STEW WITH MARC DE BOURGOGNE

Unlike many stews, which require long, slow cooking, this tasty treat from Burgundy is made in under an hour. Marc de Bourgogne and red wine are more than a match for the carp, trout and eel that are traditionally included.

SERVES 6

1.5kg/3-3⅓lb freshwater fish, such as carp, trout and skinned eel

30ml/2 tbsp plain (all-purpose) flour

50g/2oz/¼ cup butter

225g/8oz smoked bacon, cut into lardons

4 shallots, very finely chopped

225g/8oz small onions, peeled and left whole

225g/8oz/3 cups mushrooms, chopped

120ml/4fl oz/½ cup Marc de Bourgogne

1 litre/1¾ pints/4 cups red wine

300ml/½ pint/1¼ cups veal or chicken stock

1 garlic clove, crushed

1 bouquet garni

15ml/1 tbsp cornflour (cornstarch)

salt and ground black pepper

chopped fresh parsley, to garnish

garlic bread, to serve

1 Clean the fish, remove the heads and fins, fillet the flesh and cut into slices. If using eel, cut it into neat chunks.

2 Put half the flour into a plastic bag. Season with salt and pepper, then add the fish pieces and shake to coat them thoroughly.

3 In a large pan, melt the butter over a medium to high heat, then brown the fish pieces on both sides. Remove from the pan with a slotted spoon and set aside. Then add the lardons, shallots and onions to the pan and cook over a low heat for a further 10 minutes, until golden.

4 Stir in the chopped mushrooms and cook for 5 minutes more, stirring the mixture occasionally.

5 Pour in the Marc de Bourgogne, stir and flambé if you like. Add the red wine and simmer for 3–4 minutes. Stir in the stock, garlic and bouquet garni. Bring to the boil, reduce the heat and simmer for 5 minutes.

6 Add the fish and simmer for 8–10 minutes, until cooked. Using a slotted spoon, transfer the pieces of fish to a plate and keep hot. In a cup, mix the cornflour to a paste with a little cold water. Stir the paste into the pan. Bring to the boil, stirring occasionally, and cook for 5 minutes.

7 Remove the bouquet garni, then return the fish to the pan. Stir the fish gently into the sauce, then spoon into warmed bowls, garnish with the chopped parsley and serve with garlic bread.

COOK'S TIP

Lardons were originally strips of pork or bacon fat, threaded through lean meat to prevent dryness and add flavour. Today, the term is often applied to thicker strips of bacon, which are fried before being added to salads, or used in stews. Look out for packets of lardons or pancetta cubetti in the chilled food cabinet of the supermarket.

STEP 2

STEP 4

STEP 5

STEP 6

COD STEAKS WITH CREAMY SHERRY SAUCE

A molasses marinade gives these cod steaks a dusky colour that contrasts well with the creamy sherry sauce, studded with pink and green peppercorns.

SERVES 4

30ml/2 tbsp molasses

30ml/2 tbsp chopped fresh dill

30ml/2 tbsp lemon juice

4 cod steaks, each about 175g/6oz

50g/2oz/¼ cup butter

30ml/2 tbsp olive oil

3 shallots, chopped

150ml/¼ pint/⅔ cup fish stock

45ml/3 tbsp dry sherry

5ml/1 tsp drained bottled pink peppercorns, lightly crushed

5ml/1 tsp drained bottled green peppercorns, lightly crushed

3 potatoes, peeled and sliced

300ml/½ pint/1¼ cups crème fraîche

oil, for frying

3 carrots, thinly sliced

1 courgette (zucchini), thinly sliced

1 slim parsnip, thinly sliced

salt and ground black pepper

lime wedges and fresh dill sprigs, to garnish

COOK'S TIP
Always tell guests when you have included pink peppercorns in a dish. Some people are allergic to them.

1 Mix the molasses with 5ml/1 tsp salt in a small bowl. Stir in the chopped dill and lemon juice. Spread this mixture over both sides of the cod steaks. Put the fish in a shallow glass dish, cover and chill for 2 hours.

2 Heat the butter and oil in a frying pan. Add the shallots and cook until soft. Stir in the stock, sherry and both types of peppercorns. Cook for 2 minutes more.

3 Add the cod steaks to the pan and cook them for 10–12 minutes, turning once. Meanwhile, cook the potato slices in a pan of lightly salted boiling water for 5 minutes. Drain and set aside.

4 Lift the cooked fish out of the pan, place on a plate and keep hot. Stir the crème fraîche into the juices remaining in the pan, season with salt and pepper and reheat gently.

5 Deep-fry the potato slices in hot oil until golden. In a separate pan, stir-fry the carrots, courgette and parsnip in 30ml/2 tbsp hot oil for 1–2 minutes, until crisp.

6 Divide the potatoes among four plates, add the stir-fried vegetables and top with the cod and sauce. Garnish each plate with the lime wedges and sprigs of fresh dill.

STEP 2

STEP 3

STUFFED LEMON SOLE WITH SORREL AND VERMOUTH SAUCE

A mushroom and herb stuffing gives substance to sole without overwhelming the delicate flavour.
A fluffy egg sauce, spiked with vermouth, is the ideal accompaniment.

SERVES 4

115g/4oz/½ cup butter

1 small onion, finely chopped

115g/4oz/1½ cups mushrooms, finely chopped

50g/2oz/1 cup fresh brown breadcrumbs

30ml/2 tbsp chopped fresh lemon balm

4 lemon sole fillets, skinned and halved

150ml/¼ pint/⅔ cup milk

60ml/4 tbsp dry white vermouth

10ml/2 tsp lemon juice

2 egg yolks

sorrel leaves, chopped, plus some whole leaves to garnish

1 Preheat the oven to 190°C/375°F/Gas 5. Melt 25g/1oz/2 tbsp of the butter in a frying pan. Fry the onion with the mushrooms for 5–7 minutes, until the onion is golden and the mushrooms have absorbed all the liquid. Add the breadcrumbs and lemon balm to the pan and stir in, adding salt and pepper to taste.

2 Place the fillets of sole skinned side up on a board and spread some of the filling on each. Roll up the fish pieces carefully from head to tail and pack them tightly in a single layer in a shallow baking dish.

3 Pour the milk over the fish. Then cover the dish with a lid or a piece of foil, and bake in the oven for 15 minutes.

4 Heat the vermouth in a pan until it has reduced by half. Meanwhile, bring a pan of water to simmering point. Pour the reduced vermouth into a heatproof bowl, and set it over the pan of simmering water. Add the lemon juice and egg yolks and whisk over the heat until fluffy.

5 Remove from the heat and whisk while adding the remaining butter, a piece at a time. Stir in the chopped sorrel, season with salt and pepper and spoon over the fish. Garnish with sorrel leaves.

COOK'S TIP
If you cannot find lemon balm, substitute chopped lemon grass or a mixture of chopped fresh parsley and finely grated lemon rind.

PORK WITH SHERRY AND COUSCOUS

With its nutty flavour and grainy texture, couscous is the perfect partner for this lightly spiced pork dish. The sauce is rich and fruity, thanks to the raisins and dry sherry.

SERVES 4

30ml/2 tbsp plain (all-purpose) flour

500g/1¼lb boneless pork, diced

45ml/3 tbsp olive oil

1 large onion, chopped

2 garlic cloves, crushed

45ml/3 tbsp tomato purée (paste)

225g/8oz can chopped tomatoes

30ml/2 tbsp lemon juice

600ml/1 pint/2½ cups chicken stock

115g/4oz/1 cup cooked chickpeas

30ml/2 tbsp dry sherry

25g/1oz/3 tbsp raisins

175g/6oz/1½ cups couscous

50g/2oz/¼ cup butter, melted

45ml/3 tbsp chopped fresh parsley

salt and ground black pepper

1 Put the flour into a plastic bag and season with salt and pepper. Add the pork and toss to coat. Heat the oil in a flameproof casserole and fry the onion until soft. Add the pork and cook, stirring occasionally, until golden.

2 Stir in the garlic, tomato purée, tomatoes, lemon juice and stock. Season with salt and pepper. Bring to the boil, reduce the heat, cover with a lid or foil and simmer for 45 minutes. Stir in the chickpeas, sherry and raisins. Replace the cover and cook for 15 minutes more.

3 Transfer the stew to a pan over which you can place a metal colander. Line the colander with scalded muslin or cheesecloth and sprinkle in the couscous. Set the pan over a medium heat, cover the colander with a lid and cook the couscous over the stew for 30 minutes. Tip the cooked couscous into a bowl, stir in the melted butter and parsley. Use a fork to fluff up the couscous, then serve with the stew.

COOK'S TIPS
• Pork steaks are ideal for this recipe. If you use pork fillet (tenderloin), it will cook more quickly, so reduce the cooking time slightly.
• To save time, use instant couscous, of which there are several flavoured versions available. Instant couscous does not require steaming and is simply soaked in hot water. Follow the instructions on the packet.

STEP 3

LAMB WITH TARRAGON AND ARMAGNAC

A generous splash of Armagnac gives the sauce for this simple meat dish a delicious flavour
and a warm, rich colour.

SERVES 4

15ml/1 tbsp vegetable oil

25g/1oz/2 tbsp butter

12 lamb noisettes (trimmed eye of loin or rib)

45ml/3 tbsp Armagnac

45ml/3 tbsp dry white wine

300ml/½ pint/1¼ cups lamb or chicken stock

10ml/2 tsp chopped fresh tarragon

salt and ground black pepper

fresh tarragon sprigs, to garnish

1 Heat the oil with half the butter in a frying pan. Season the noisettes with pepper. When the butter has melted, add the noisettes of lamb to the pan and fry them over a high heat until they are browned on both sides.

2 Lower the heat and fry the lamb until cooked to taste. The lamb can be served pink, or cooked through, but take care not to overcook it, or it will be dry. Using tongs, transfer the noisettes to a plate and keep them hot while making the sauce.

3 Drain the excess oil from the frying pan and add the Armagnac. Flambé it, if you like. Stir in the white wine. Place over a medium to high heat until the liquid has reduced to three-quarters of its original volume.

4 Stir in the lamb or chicken stock and chopped tarragon. Bring to the boil, reduce the heat and simmer for 3–4 minutes. Stir in the remaining butter and season if necessary. Serve the noisettes with the sauce, and garnish with the tarragon.

COOK'S TIP

Noisettes are rounds of boneless lamb, cut from the loins or fillets on either side of the saddle and tied with string (twine). Most butchers sell them or will cut them to order. The string can be removed and the noisettes stuffed with chopped fresh herbs, smoked oysters or tapenade (olive paste). Retie before cooking.

WHISKY CHICKEN

As every good Scot knows, honey and whisky go very well together. Add sesame seeds, and you will have a chicken coating that is absolutely delicious.

SERVES 4

25g/1oz/4 tbsp sesame seeds, crushed

2 garlic cloves, crushed

pinch of paprika

60ml/4 tbsp oil

30ml/2 tbsp whisky

30ml/2 tbsp clear honey

4 chicken portions

2 large onions, finely sliced

1 green (bell) pepper, seeded and sliced

150ml/¼ pint/⅔ cup vegetable stock

1 Preheat the oven to 190°C/375°F/Gas 5. In a small bowl, mix the sesame seeds with the garlic and paprika. Stir in half the oil, then add the whisky and honey. Stir in a little water if the mixture is too thick.

2 Make several cuts in the chicken portions and arrange them in a single layer in a baking dish. Spread the paste over. Roast for 40 minutes, or until the chicken is cooked through.

3 Meanwhile, heat the remaining oil in a frying pan and fry the onion slices over a medium heat for 15 minutes, or until softened and beginning to brown. Add the green pepper and fry for 5 minutes more.

4 Stir in the stock, season with salt and pepper and cook gently for about 20 minutes, stirring from time to time. Serve warm with the cooked chicken.

VARIATION

Instead of making cuts in the chicken portions, ease the skin away from the flesh and push the paste underneath. This keeps the flesh wonderfully moist.

CHICKEN WITH WILD MUSHROOMS AND VERMOUTH

Tender chicken slices, simmered in a rich sour cream sauce spiked with vermouth, make a dish worthy of the most sophisticated dinner party.

SERVES 4

30ml/2 tbsp oil

1 leek, finely chopped

4 chicken breast portions, sliced

225g/8oz/3 cups wild mushrooms, sliced if large

15ml/1 tbsp brandy

pinch of freshly grated nutmeg

1.5ml/¼ tsp chopped, fresh thyme

150ml/¼ pint/⅔ cup dry white vermouth

150ml/¼ pint/⅔ cup chicken stock

6 pitted green olives, quartered

150ml/¼ pint/⅔ cup sour cream

salt and ground black pepper

fresh thyme sprigs and croutons, to garnish

1 Heat the oil in a frying pan and fry the chopped leek over a medium heat for 4–5 minutes until softened but not browned. Add the chicken slices and mushrooms. Fry, stirring occasionally, until the chicken is cooked through and is starting to brown.

2 Pour over the brandy and ignite. When the flames have died down, stir in the nutmeg, thyme, vermouth and stock, with salt and pepper to taste.

3 Bring to the boil, reduce the heat and simmer for 5 minutes. Stir in the olives and most of the sour cream. Reheat gently, but do not let the mixture boil. Garnish with the remaining sour cream, the thyme sprigs and the croutons.

COOK'S TIP

Using dried wild mushrooms, as well as fresh, intensifies the flavour of this dish still more. Soak them in warm water for 20 minutes before use. The water used for soaking can be strained and substituted for some of the stock.

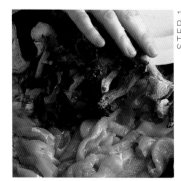

STEP 1

RABBIT WITH PUY LENTILS AND PORT

Port gives this rustic dish from France a wonderfully warm and robust flavour.

SERVES 4

15ml/1 tbsp plain (all-purpose) flour

450g/1lb diced boneless rabbit

15ml/1 tbsp olive oil

2 onions, sliced

1 garlic clove, crushed

225g/8oz/3 cups mushrooms, sliced

45ml/3 tbsp port

400ml/14fl oz/1⅔ cups chicken or vegetable stock

5ml/1 tsp red wine or balsamic vinegar

30ml/2 tbsp chopped fresh parsley, plus extra to garnish

15ml/1 tbsp tomato purée (paste)

175g/6oz/¾ cup Puy lentils

12 slices French bread

30ml/2 tbsp tapenade (olive paste)

15g/½oz/1 tbsp butter

salt and ground black pepper

1 Preheat the oven to 180°C/350°F/Gas 4. Put the flour into a plastic bag, season with salt and pepper and add the rabbit. Shake to coat evenly.

2 Heat the oil in a flameproof casserole and fry the rabbit until browned.

3 Stir in the sliced onions, garlic and mushrooms. Add the port, stock, vinegar, parsley and tomato purée. Stir well, then bring the mixture to the boil. Cover the casserole with a lid, transfer it to the oven and cook for 40 minutes.

4 Meanwhile, bring a pan of water to the boil, add the lentils and cook for 35 minutes, until tender.

5 Spread the French bread with the tapenade. Drain the lentils, stir them into the casserole and put the bread on top, tapenade side up. Dot with butter. Return the casserole to the oven, uncovered, and cook for 10 minutes. Serve at once, garnished with the extra chopped parsley.

VARIATIONS

• Pork fillet (tenderloin) can be used instead of rabbit. Diced chicken could also be used. To give either of these a more gamey flavour, add 15–30ml/1–2 tbsp crushed juniper berries.

• Use Madeira instead of port, if you prefer.

STEP 3

VENISON STEAKS with DRAMBUIE and CELERIAC

Some marinades are discarded after use, but this one, based on Drambuie and apple juice, is just too good to throw away. It forms the basis of a sauce that tastes wonderful with the tender venison steaks.

SERVES 4

4 venison steaks, each about 176g/6oz (see Cook's Tip)

1 small celeriac

oil, for deep-frying

25g/1oz/¼ cup plain (all-purpose) flour

300ml/½ pint/1¼ cups game or chicken stock

salt and ground black pepper

fresh thyme sprigs, to garnish

for the marinade

45ml/3 tbsp Drambuie

45ml/3 tbsp oil

30ml/2 tbsp apple juice

1 bay leaf

2 fresh thyme sprigs

2 juniper berries, crushed

1 Make the marinade by mixing all the ingredients in a large bowl and stirring in salt and pepper to taste. Add the venison steaks, turning to coat them in the mixture. Cover and chill for 3 hours or overnight.

2 Peel the celeriac and slice it thinly. Fry the slices in hot oil until crisp. Remove with a slotted spoon, drain on kitchen paper and keep hot.

3 Lift the steaks out of the marinade and dry them with kitchen paper. Carefully pour off most of the oil from the frying pan, leaving just enough to shallow-fry the steaks. Add them to the pan and fry for 4 minutes on each side. Transfer the cooked steaks to a platter and keep them hot.

4 Strain the marinade into a pitcher and stir in the flour to make a smooth paste. Stir into the pan with the stock and season with salt and pepper. Bring to the boil, stirring constantly, and cook for 2 minutes.

5 Divide the celeriac crisps among individual plates and add a venison steak to each. Spoon over the sauce, garnish with thyme and serve.

COOK'S TIP
Farmed venison steaks are young and will cook quickly. If you buy wild venison, it may well need to be cooked for considerably longer. Simmer it in the marinade for about 45 minutes.

STEP 1

PASTRY BOXES with SPRING VEGETABLES in PERNOD SAUCE

For a vegetarian dish that looks spectacular and tastes superb, these puff pastry cases filled with early
vegetables and surrounded by a piquant Pernod and tomato sauce are difficult to beat.

SERVES 4

225g/8oz puff pastry, thawed if frozen

15ml/1 tbsp grated Parmesan cheese

15ml/1 tbsp chopped fresh parsley

beaten egg, to glaze

175g/6oz podded fresh broad (fava) beans

115g/4oz baby carrots, scraped

4 baby leeks, cleaned

75g/3oz/generous ½ cup peas, thawed if frozen

50g/2oz/½ cup mangetouts (snow peas), trimmed

salt and ground black pepper

fresh dill sprigs, to garnish

for the sauce

200g/7oz can chopped tomatoes

25g/1oz/2 tbsp butter

25g/1oz/¼ cup plain (all-purpose) flour

pinch of granulated sugar

45ml/3 tbsp chopped fresh dill

300ml/½ pint/1¼ cups water

15ml/1 tbsp Pernod

COOK'S TIP
If there is time, at step 2,
chill the pastry shapes for
20 minutes before baking.

1 Preheat the oven to 220ºC/425ºF/Gas 7. Lightly grease a baking sheet. Roll out the pastry very thinly. Sprinkle the cheese and parsley over, fold and roll once more, then cut out four 10 x 7.5cm/ 4 x 3in rectangles.

2 Lift the rectangles on to the baking sheet. With a sharp knife, cut an inner rectangle about 1cm/½in from the edge of each pastry shape, cutting halfway through. Score criss-cross lines on top of the inner rectangle, brush with egg and bake for 12–15 minutes, until golden.

3 Meanwhile, make the sauce. Press the tomatoes through a sieve into a pan, add the remaining ingredients and bring to the boil, stirring all the time. Season with salt and pepper, reduce the heat and simmer until needed.

4 Cook the broad beans in a pan of lightly salted boiling water for about 8 minutes. Add the carrots, leeks and peas, cook for 5 minutes more, than add the mangetouts. Cook for 1 minute. Drain all the vegetables very well.

5 Using a knife, loosen the notched squares and lift them out from the pastry boxes. Spoon the vegetables into the pastry cases, pour the sauce over, pop the pastry lids on top and serve, garnished with dill.

POLENTA TRIANGLES WITH SPICED RED CABBAGE

Calvados is the special ingredient that transforms this tasty vegetable dish. It is particularly good with apples and red cabbage.

SERVES 4

25g/1oz/2 tbsp butter

15ml/1 tbsp olive oil

1 onion, sliced

1 garlic clove, crushed

1 red cabbage, about 450g/1lb, shredded

250ml/8fl oz/1 cup vegetable stock

45ml/3 tbsp red wine vinegar

45ml/3 tbsp clear honey

15ml/1 tbsp lemon juice

pinch of ground cloves

2 cooking apples

30ml/2 tbsp Calvados

salt and ground black pepper

sprigs of fresh flat leaf parsley, to garnish

for the polenta

475ml/16fl oz/2 cups water

5ml/1 tsp salt

175g/6oz/1 cup polenta

50g/2oz/¼ cup butter, diced

30ml/2 tbsp grated Parmesan cheese

45ml/3 tbsp chopped fresh herbs

olive oil, for brushing

25g/1oz/⅓ cup pine nuts, crushed

COOK'S TIPS
• Red cabbage tastes better the day after it is cooked, so this is a good dish for cooking ahead.
• If you don't want to use the oven, brush the polenta with oil and grill (broil), turning once.

1 Start by making the polenta. Bring the water to the boil in a large pan. Add the salt, pour in the polenta and cook for about 8 minutes, stirring constantly with a wooden spoon, until the mixture resembles thick porridge. Do not let it stick to the bottom of the pan.

2 Remove the polenta from the heat and stir in the butter, Parmesan cheese and herbs. Spread the polenta about 1cm/½in thick on a flat plate and cover with foil or clear film (plastic wrap). Cool, then chill.

3 Preheat the oven to 190°C/375°F/Gas 5. Heat the butter and olive oil in a large frying pan. Fry the onion until golden, then add all the remaining ingredients, except the apples and Calvados. Bring to the boil, reduce the heat, cover and simmer for 40 minutes. Stir the mixture occasionally and add a little water if it becomes too dry.

4 Peel, core and chop the apples. Stir them into the red cabbage mixture, pour over the Calvados and season to taste. Simmer for 15 minutes.

5 Cut the polenta into triangles. Grease a baking sheet and arrange the polenta triangles on top. Brush with oil, sprinkle with the nuts and bake for 15–20 minutes until golden brown. Arrange around the rim of a heated serving platter and pile the red cabbage in the centre. Garnish with the parsley and serve.

CRÊPES SUZETTE WITH COINTREAU AND COGNAC

It is not surprising that the popularity of this classic dessert has endured. Filling crêpes with a rich orange and Cointreau butter and flaming them with cognac is a certain recipe for success.

SERVES 6

115g/4oz/1 cup plain (all-purpose) flour

2.5ml/½ tsp salt

2 eggs, beaten

300ml/½ pint/1¼ cups milk

oil, for frying

juice of 2 oranges

45ml/3 tbsp cognac

icing (confectioners') sugar for dusting

strips of thinly pared orange rind, to decorate

for the orange butter

175g/6oz/¾ cup butter, softened

50g/2oz/¼ cup granulated sugar

grated rind of 2 oranges

30ml/2 tbsp Cointreau

WARNING
Take great care when heating alcohol in the kitchen, because splashes of scalding liquid and flame can be hazardous.

1 Start by making the orange butter. Cream the butter in a bowl. Gradually add the sugar, beating after each addition, then stir in the orange rind and Cointreau. Set aside in a cool place – but not in the refrigerator – while you make the batter for the crêpes.

2 Sift the flour and salt into a bowl, make a well in the centre and add the beaten eggs. Stir the liquid, gradually incorporating the surrounding flour mixture. When smooth, add the milk gradually and beat to a smooth batter. Pour into a pitcher.

3 Heat the oil in a 15cm/6in crêpe or pancake pan and pour in a little batter. Tilt the pan so that the batter spreads to cover the pan thinly. Cook until the underside of the crêpe is golden, then turn or flip it over and cook the other side. Slide the crêpe out of the pan. Make at least five more crêpes with the remaining batter.

4 Spread the crêpes with half the orange butter and fold each one in half, then in half again.

5 Heat the rest of the orange butter with the orange juice in a large, heavy frying pan. Add the

folded pancakes and spoon the sauce over. Simmer the crêpes in the sauce for 3 or 4 minutes to heat them through.

6 Push the crêpes to one side of the pan and pour in the cognac. Heat, then carefully set the alcohol alight. When the flames die down, spoon the sauce over the pancakes again. Serve immediately, dusted with icing sugar and decorated with strips of orange rind.

COOK'S TIP
You may find it easier to heat the cognac in a metal soup ladle, then ignite it and pour it carefully over the crêpes in the pan.

VARIATION
Not traditional, but just as delicious, is to use rum in place of the Cointreau and cognac, and add sliced fresh pineapple and a little toasted coconut.

STEP 3

STEP 4

STEP 5

SOUFFLÉS WITH GRAND MARNIER ICE CREAM

Dip a spoon into one of these delicious desserts and experience a delightful contrast in texture and temperature. Hot, light Grand Marnier soufflés are teamed with ice cream flavoured with the same orange liqueur.

SERVES 6

40g/1½oz/3 tbsp butter

40g/1½oz/⅓ cup plain (all purpose) flour

250ml/8fl oz/1 cup milk

40g/1½oz/3 tbsp caster (superfine) sugar

30ml/2 tbsp Grand Marnier

5 eggs, separated

icing (confectioners') sugar, for dusting

for the ice cream

150ml/¼ pint/⅔ cup double (heavy) cream

30ml/2 tbsp Grand Marnier

30ml/2 tbsp orange juice

10ml/2 tsp icing (confectioners') sugar

1 Make the ice cream. Mix the cream, Grand Marnier, orange juice and icing sugar in a small bowl. Churn in an ice-cream maker or spoon into a freezerproof bowl and freeze for 30 minutes, or until ice crystals begin to form around the edge. Stir well, return to the freezer and freeze until firm.

2 Using two spoons, shape the frozen Grand Marnier ice cream into six small ovals. Place on a plate and freeze again until solid.

3 Preheat the oven to 200°C/400°F/Gas 6. Lightly grease six small soufflé dishes. Melt the butter in a heavy pan, stir in the flour and cook for 1 minute. Gradually add the milk, stirring constantly until the mixture boils and thickens. Cook for 2 minutes, then remove from the heat. Cool slightly, then beat in the sugar, Grand Marnier and egg yolks.

4 Whisk the egg whites in a large bowl until stiff. Using a metal spoon, fold them into the Grand Marnier mixture.

5 Spoon the mixture into the soufflé dishes, stand on a baking sheet and bake for 25–35 minutes, until the soufflés have risen and are lightly browned on top.

6 Quickly dust with icing sugar, make a hole in the top of each soufflé and add a spoonful of Grand Marnier ice cream. Serve at once.

COOK'S TIP

The bowl and whisk used for whisking the egg whites must be grease-free.

SHERRY TRIFLE

Here is one recipe that really doesn't need an introduction. There are many versions of this cold dessert
laced with sherry, and this is one of the most luxurious.

SERVES 6–8

**75g/3oz ratafia biscuits
(almond macaroons)**

90ml/6 tbsp raspberry jam

175ml/6fl oz/³⁄₄ cup sherry

175g/6oz/1 cup raspberries

**225g/8oz/1 cup seedless black
grapes, halved**

**300ml/¹⁄₂ pint/1¹⁄₄ cups double
(heavy) cream, whipped**

**crystallized fruit and icing
(confectioners') sugar**

for the custard

**25g/1oz/¹⁄₄ cup cornflour
(cornstarch)**

600ml/1 pint/2¹⁄₂ cups milk

3 egg yolks

**2.5ml/¹⁄₂ tsp vanilla essence
(extract)**

**25g/1oz/2 tbsp caster
(superfine) sugar**

VARIATIONS
• If you prefer, echo the almond
flavour of the ratafia biscuits by
using amaretto liqueur, or use
your favourite liqueur instead
of sherry.
• Vary the fruit filling to make
the most of seasonal
availability.

1 Prepare the custard. In a heatproof bowl, blend
the cornflour with a little of the milk. Then stir
in the egg yolks, vanilla essence and sugar. Pour
the remaining milk into a pan and bring to the
boil. Then pour the boiled milk on to the
cornflour mixture, stirring constantly. Transfer the
mixture back into the pan, bring to the boil, then
lower the heat and simmer for 3 minutes. Return
to the bowl, cover the surface with baking
parchment and put aside to cool.

2 Sandwich the ratafia biscuits together with the
jam, then arrange them in a deep glass bowl.
Sprinkle the sherry over the biscuits.

3 Spoon half the custard over the biscuits. Level
the surface and arrange the fruit on top. Cover the
fruit with the remaining custard, making sure that
the layers are visible through the sides of the
bowl. Then swirl or pipe the cream over the trifle
and decorate with crystallized fruit. Dust lightly
with icing sugar just before serving.

COOK'S TIP
If you make sure the paper touches the surface of
the custard, this will ensure it does not form a
skin as it cools.

ZABAGLIONE

This gloriously creamy, classic Italian dessert owes its rich flavour to Marsala, a Sicilian fortified wine.

SERVES 4

2 sponge fingers, crumbled
90ml/6 tbsp Marsala
6 fresh apricots, stoned (pitted) and sliced
5 egg yolks
50g/2oz/¼ cup caster (superfine) sugar

1 Divide the crumbled sponge fingers among four heatproof dessert glasses. Sprinkle 15ml/1 tbsp of the Marsala over the crumbled sponge. Set aside eight of the apricot slices for decoration and divide the rest among the glasses.

2 Put the egg yolks in a heatproof bowl. Whisk them lightly, then whisk in the sugar and the remaining Marsala.

3 Set the bowl over a pan of barely simmering water and continue to whisk until the mixture is very thick and creamy. When you lift the whisk out of the bowl, the trail should remain visible on the surface for 2–3 seconds.

4 Pour the zabaglione into the glasses and decorate with the reserved apricot slices. Serve while still warm.

VARIATION
Try using madeira instead of marsala. Crumbled macaroons are a good substitute for sponge fingers.

POACHED MANDARINS WITH SHORTBREAD LEAVES

Whole mandarins macerated in a liqueur-flavoured syrup make a superb sweet.

SERVES 4

225g/8oz/generous 1 cup soft light brown sugar
750ml/1¼ pints/3 cups water
12 small mandarin oranges
45ml/3 tbsp Mandarine Napoléon liqueur
15ml/1 tbsp lemon juice
whipped cream, to serve

for the shortbread
50g/2oz/¼ cup butter, softened
75g/3oz/⅔ cup plain (all-purpose) flour, sifted
25g/1oz/2 tbsp caster (superfine) sugar, plus extra for sprinkling
5ml/1 tsp finely grated lemon rind

1 Preheat the oven to 160°C/325°F/Gas 3. Grease a baking sheet. Make the shortbread. Put the butter, flour, sugar and lemon rind in a large bowl and knead together until smooth and silky.

2 Roll out on a lightly floured surface to a thickness of 5mm/¼in. Cut out leaf shapes by hand or with a biscuit cutter. Lift on to the baking sheet and bake for 15 minutes. Sprinkle with caster sugar and leave to cool on the baking sheet for 5 minutes before removing.

3 Mix the brown sugar and water in a large pan. Heat until the sugar has dissolved, bring to the boil, then cook until reduced by half. Lower the heat so that the syrup barely simmers.

4 Peel the mandarins and remove any pith. Stir the liqueur and lemon juice into the syrup, add the mandarins, cover and cook gently for 40 minutes. Leave to cool. Serve with the shortbread leaves, and offer whipped cream to those who want it.

COOK'S TIP
Store the biscuits (cookies) in an airtight tin. If you add a few grains of rice to the tin, this will absorb moisture and prevent them from softening.

STEP 1

STEP 3

STEP 2

TIA MARIA GATEAU

Serve this rich gateau as a dessert, or with small cups of espresso for an afternoon treat. The Tia Maria cream filling is positively decadent.

SERVES 6-8

150g/5oz/1¼ cups self-raising (self-rising) flour

25g/1oz/¼ cup cocoa powder (unsweetened)

7.5ml/1½ tsp baking powder

3 eggs, beaten

175g/6oz/¾ cup butter, softened

175g/6oz/¾ cup caster (superfine) sugar

50g/2oz/½ cup chopped walnuts

walnut brittle, to decorate (see Cook's Tip)

for the filling and coating

600ml/1 pint/2½ cups double (heavy) cream

45ml/3 tbsp Tia Maria

50g/2oz/⅔ cup desiccated (dry unsweetened shredded) coconut, toasted

1 Preheat the oven to 160°C/325°F/Gas 3. Grease and base-line two sandwich cake tins (layer cake pans). Sift the flour, cocoa powder and baking powder into a large bowl. Add the eggs, butter, sugar and walnuts and mix thoroughly, either with a wooden spoon or with a hand-held electric mixer, until the mixture is light and fluffy.

2 Divide the mixture between the cake tins, level the surface of each and bake for 35–40 minutes, until risen and browned. Remove the cakes from the tins and leave to cool on a wire rack.

3 Make the filling by putting the cream in a bowl, slowly adding the Tia Maria, and whisking until the mixture forms soft peaks.

4 Slice each cake horizontally in half to make four layers. Sandwich together with flavoured cream.

5 Coat the sides of the cake with cream. Spread the toasted coconut on baking parchment. Then, hold the top and bottom of the cake and turn it on its side and roll in the coconut until evenly coated. Put the cake on a serving plate, spread more cream over the top and pipe the remainder around the rim. Decorate with walnut brittle.

COOK'S TIP

To make walnut brittle, slowly heat 75g/3oz/6 tbsp caster sugar in a pan. When the sugar has dissolved, stir in 50g/2oz/½ cup broken walnuts. Turn the mixture on to a sheet of baking parchment and leave to set. Break the brittle into pieces with a rolling pin.

STEP 3

APRICOT FRANGIPANE TART WITH KIRSCH

Baking a tart in a rectangular case makes it very easy to cut. This one has light, lime-flavoured pastry filled with almond sponge laced with kirsch. Topped with apricots and crushed macaroons, it tastes sensational warm or at room temperature.

SERVES 6

225g/8oz/2 cups plain (all-purpose) flour

115g/4oz/½ cup butter

10ml/2 tbsp finely grated lime rind

12 fresh apricots, stoned (pitted), some halved, some thinly sliced

75g/3oz ratafia biscuits (almond macaroons), crushed

natural (plain) yogurt or cream, to serve

for the filling

25g/1oz/2 tbsp butter, softened

30ml/2 tbsp soft light brown sugar

15ml/1 tbsp plain (all-purpose) flour

50g/2oz/½ cup ground almonds

1 egg, beaten

45ml/3 tbsp kirsch

COOK'S TIP
If the pastry is sticky and hard to handle, roll it out between sheets of baking parchment.

1 Sift the flour into a mixing bowl, then rub (cut) in the butter until the mixture resembles breadcrumbs. Stir in the grated lime rind and add enough cold water to make a soft dough. Wrap in clear film (plastic wrap) and chill for 30 minutes.

2 Meanwhile, make the filling. Cream the butter with the soft light brown sugar, then stir in the flour, ground almonds, egg and kirsch. Preheat the oven to 200°C/400°F/Gas 6.

3 Roll out the pastry on a lightly floured surface to a 40 x 15cm/16 x 6in rectangle and use this to line a 35 x 11.5cm/14 x 4½in rectangular flan tin (quiche pan).

4 Spread the filling in the pastry case and arrange the apricot halves and slices, cut side down, on top. Scatter over the crushed ratafia biscuits. Bake for 35–40 minutes until the pastry is golden. Serve warm or cold, with yogurt or cream.

STEP 4

FRAMBOISE SABAYON
with BERRIES

This dessert is a simple combination of beautiful summer
berries and a caramelized creamy topping,
and it tastes superb.

SERVES 4

115g/4oz/1 cup fresh blueberries

175g/6oz/1 cup fresh
raspberries

3 egg yolks

25g/1oz/2 tbsp caster
(superfine) sugar

60ml/4 tbsp framboise

extra sugar, for topping

1 Arrange the fresh blueberries and raspberries in wide, flameproof
soup bowls or on flameproof dessert plates.

2 Half fill a pan with water and bring to the simmering point. Put the
yolks and sugar in a large, heatproof bowl that will fit over the pan.

3 Place the bowl over the water, pour in the framboise and whisk
the mixture until it is thick and foamy. Preheat the grill (broiler).

4 Spoon the sabayon sauce over the fruits, sprinkle with a little sugar
and flash briefly under the grill so that the sugar caramelizes and
turns golden.

VARIATION
In the winter, when fresh soft fruits are difficult to come by, try this
with dried apricots macerated in brandy and topped with Greek
(US strained plain) yogurt.

STEP 1

STEP 3

AMARETTO
ICE CREAM

Asked to name their favourite liqueur, many people would
plump for Amaretto. Its rich almond flavour makes for a
wonderful ice cream.

SERVES 4-6

750ml/1¼ pints/3 cups good
quality vanilla ice cream,
softened

30ml/2 tbsp amaretto liqueur

15ml/1 tbsp orange juice

1.5ml/¼ tsp vanilla essence
(extract)

thinly pared orange rind, to
decorate

for the brandy-snap baskets

50g/2oz/¼ cup butter

50g/2oz/¼ cup caster
(superfine) sugar

75g/3oz/⅓ cup golden syrup
(light corn syrup)

5ml/1 tsp ground ginger

grated rind and juice of 1 lemon

50g/2oz/½ cup plain
(all-purpose) flour

1 Preheat the oven to 180°C/350°F/Gas 4. Line three baking sheets
with baking parchment.

2 Beat the ice cream until soft and creamy, then beat in the amaretto,
orange juice and vanilla essence. Return to the tub or a similar
container for freezing. Freeze until firm.

3 Put the butter, sugar, syrup and ground ginger into a pan. Heat
gently, stirring constantly until the butter has melted, then switch off
the heat and stir in the lemon rind and juice, and then the flour.

4 The mixture hardens quickly, so only bake two biscuits (cookies) at
a time. Put spoonfuls of the
mixture on the baking sheets.
Bake for 10–12 minutes, until
golden. Cool for a few seconds.

5 Lift each biscuit with a palette
knife or spatula and drape over a
small orange or an upturned cup.
Leave to cool and harden, then
invert on to plates. Add scoops
of amaretto ice cream and
decorate with orange rind.

STEP 5

COFFEE AND KAHLÚA MACADAMIA CREAMS

These rich creams have a wonderfully intense flavour, and meringue fingers are the perfect accompaniment.

SERVES 4-6

10ml/2 tsp powdered gelatine

45ml/3 tbsp water

350ml/12fl oz/1½ cups double (heavy) cream

150ml/¼ pint/⅔ cup thick natural (plain) yogurt

15ml/1 tbsp strong black coffee

25g/1oz/¼ cup icing (confectioners') sugar

15ml/1 tbsp **Kahlúa** liqueur

50g/2oz/½ cup macadamia nuts, toasted and chopped

roasted macadamia nuts and chocolate coffee beans, to decorate

for the meringue fingers

1 egg white

50g/2oz/¼ cup caster (superfine) sugar

1 Preheat the oven to 120°C/250°F/Gas ½. Cover a baking sheet with baking parchment. To make the meringue fingers, whisk the egg white in a grease-free bowl until stiff and dry. Whisk in half the sugar until stiff, then fold in the remaining sugar. Put the meringue mixture into a piping (icing) bag fitted with a star nozzle or tip. Pipe finger shapes of meringue on to the baking sheet. Bake for 2½ hours, or until crisp.

2 Meanwhile, make the creams. Sprinkle the gelatine over the water in a small heatproof bowl. When spongy, stir over simmering water until dissolved.

3 Combine the cream, yogurt, coffee, icing sugar and liqueur in a bowl. Mix well, then stir in the dissolved gelatine mixture. Chill until on the point of setting, then stir in the nuts and spoon into small moulds. Chill further until firm, unmould and decorate with nuts and chocolate coffee beans. Serve with the meringue fingers.

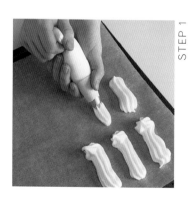
STEP 1

MARASCHINO CRÈME BRÛLÉE

Crack the crunchy topping to discover rich liqueur-soaked fruits under a cream blanket.

SERVES 6

6 eggs, lightly beaten

300ml/½ pint/1¼ cups milk

300ml/½ pint/1¼ cups double (heavy) cream, lightly whipped

50g/2oz/¼ cup caster (superfine) sugar

5ml/1 tsp rose water

50g/2oz/½ cup pitted cherries, halved

50g/2oz/½ cup seedless grapes, halved

15ml/1 tsp maraschino liqueur

75g/3oz/½ cup soft light brown sugar

whole fresh cherries, to serve

1 Mix the eggs and milk in a large heatproof bowl. Place over a pan of barely simmering water and whisk until the mixture thickens to a light custard.

2 Fold in the cream, sugar and rose water. Remove the pan from the heat and leave to cool.

3 Divide the fruit among six flameproof dishes. Sprinkle the maraschino liqueur over the fruit and spoon the custard on top. Preheat the grill (broiler).

4 Sprinkle the sugar over the custard in an even layer. Stand the dishes under the grill until the sugar caramelizes. Serve hot or cold, with whole cherries.

STEP 1

STEP 3

SERVES 10–12

50g/2oz/⅓ cup sultanas (golden raisins)

175g/6oz/1 cup ready-to-eat dried pineapple, chopped

175g/6oz/1 cup ready-to-eat dried papaya, chopped

175g/6oz/1 cup ready-to-eat dried mango, chopped

60ml/4 tbsp rum

225g/8oz/1 cup butter, softened

225g/8oz/1⅓ cups soft light brown sugar

4 eggs, beaten

225g/8oz/2 cups plain (all-purpose) flour, sifted with 10ml/2 tsp mixed spice (apple pie spice)

for the topping

75g/3oz/1 cup desiccated (dry shredded unsweetened) coconut

50g/2oz/⅓ cup ready-to-eat dried papaya, chopped

50g/2oz/⅓ cup ready-to-eat dried pineapple, chopped

COOK'S TIP
If the cake mixture starts to curdle as the egg is added, stir in a little of the cake mixture.

STEP 5

CARIBBEAN RUM CAKE

This marvellously moist fruit cake is filled with tropical fruits, rum and coconut.

1 Combine the sultanas with the dried pineapple, papaya and mango in a glass bowl. Spoon the rum over the fruit, cover and leave for a day, or just a few hours if that is all the time available.

2 Preheat the oven to 180°C/350°F/Gas 4. Grease and line a 20cm/8in round cake tin (pan).

3 Cream the butter with the brown sugar until light and fluffy. Beat in the eggs, adding a little at a time so the mixture does not curdle.

4 Fold in the flour and spice mixture, then stir in the soaked fruits. Mix thoroughly, spoon into the tin and level the surface.

5 In a small bowl, mix the coconut, papaya and pineapple for the topping. Sprinkle over the top of the cake. Bake for 1½–1¾ hours, or until a skewer inserted in the cake comes out clean. Cover with foil if the top begins to brown too much. Leave the cake in the tin for 15 minutes before transferring it to a wire rack to cool completely.

GINGER AND PEACH CAKE WITH PEACH SCHNAPPS

At the centre of this spicy cake is a luscious layer of peaches and peach-flavoured spirit.

SERVES 8

225g/8oz/2 cups plain (all-purpose) flour

7.5ml/1½ tsp baking powder

10ml/2 tsp ground ginger

175g/6oz/¾ cup butter

175g/6oz/¾ cup caster (superfine) sugar

3 eggs, beaten

3 peaches, stoned (pitted) and sliced

45ml/3 tbsp peach schnapps

for the topping

25g/1oz/2 tbsp butter

25g/1oz/¼ cup plain (all-purpose) flour

30ml/2 tbsp caster (superfine) sugar

50g/2oz/½ cup flaked almonds, crushed

VARIATION

Use nectarines or plums instead of peaches, or try pitted cherries with kirsch.

1 Preheat the oven to 180°C/350°F/Gas 4. Grease and line a 20cm/8in springform cake tin (pan). Sift the flour, baking powder and ground ginger into a bowl. In a separate bowl, cream the butter with the sugar until light and fluffy. Beat in the eggs, a little at a time.

2 Fold in the flour and spices and mix thoroughly. Spoon half the mixture into the cake tin. Arrange the peach slices in concentric circles on top. Pour over the peach schnapps and cover with the remaining cake mixture.

3 Make the topping in a small bowl. Rub (cut) the butter into the flour, then stir in the sugar and almonds. Sprinkle the topping evenly over the surface of the cake and bake for 1¼–1½ hours, or until cooked.

STEP 2

115g/4oz/½ cup butter

200g/7oz/scant 1 cup granulated sugar

3 eggs

200g/7oz/1¾ cups strong white bread flour

pinch of salt

10ml/2 tsp easy-blend (fast-acting) dried yeast

grated rind of 2 oranges

3 slices glacé (candied) orange, chopped

few drops of vanilla essence (extract)

15ml/1 tbsp orange juice

30ml/2 tbsp Curaçao

5 thin orange slices, peel and pith removed

5ml/1 tsp clear honey

COOK'S TIP
If you prefer a more traditional cake shape, bake the mixture in an 18cm/7in round cake tin (pan).

STEP 4

ORANGE CAKE WITH CURAÇAO

A celebration of citrus, this rich, sweet yeast cake is flavoured with orange rind and juice, glacé orange and Curaçao.

1 Grease and base-line a 900g/2lb loaf tin (pan). In a bowl, cream the butter with the sugar until soft and fluffy. Beat in the eggs, a little at a time.

2 In another bowl, sift the flour and salt together and stir in the easy-blend yeast.

3 Stir the creamed mixture into the flour, add the orange rind, chopped glacé orange, vanilla essence, orange juice and liqueur and mix

thoroughly. Spoon the mixture into the prepared tin, then cover and leave in a warm place for 1 hour. Preheat the oven to 190°C/375°F/Gas 5.

4 Overlap the orange slices on top of the cake mixture and bake in the middle of the oven for 45–55 minutes, or until cooked. Remove from the oven and immediately brush the orange slices with the honey. Leave to cool in the tin for 10 minutes before removing.

MINI FLORENTINES WITH GRAND MARNIER

The addition of a dash of orange liqueur gives these ever-popular nut, dried fruit and chocolate biscuits a touch of luxury and richness.

MAKES ABOUT 24

50g/2oz/⅓ cup soft light brown sugar

15ml/1 tbsp clear honey

15ml/1 tbsp Grand Marnier

50g/2oz/¼ cup butter

40g/1½ oz/6 tbsp plain (all-purpose) flour

25g/1oz/¼ cup hazelnuts, roughly chopped

50g/2oz/½ cup flaked almonds, chopped

50g/2oz/¼ cup glacé (candied) cherries, chopped

115g/4oz dark chocolate, melted, for coating

1 Preheat the oven to 180°C/350°F/Gas 4. Then, line three or four baking sheets with baking parchment. Combine the sugar, honey, liqueur and butter in a small pan and melt gently over a low heat.

2 Remove the pan from the heat and tip in the flour, hazelnuts, almonds and glacé cherries. Stir together thoroughly.

3 Spoon small heaps of the mixture on to the baking sheets, making sure they are well spaced. Bake for about 10 minutes, until golden brown.

4 Leave the biscuits (cookies) on the baking sheets to harden a little, then lift them carefully and put them on a wire rack to cool.

5 Spread the melted chocolate evenly over one side of each florentine. As the chocolate begins to set, drag a fork across it to decorate with wavy lines. Leave to set completely.

VARIATION
For an extra decoration, pour melted chocolate into a paper piping bag, snip a small hole in the end and pipe zigzag lines over the plain side of each florentine.

COOK'S TIP
Melt the chocolate in a heatproof bowl sitting over a pan of water that has recently boiled, but that has been removed from the heat.

BOURBON BALLS

This American speciality laces a delicious crumb and pecan mixture with bourbon.

MAKES ABOUT 25

175g/6oz **N**ice biscuits or similar plain vanilla biscuits (cookies)

115g/4oz/1 cup pecan nuts, chopped

30ml/2 tbsp cocoa powder (unsweetened)

75g/3oz/¾ cup icing (confectioners') sugar, sifted

30ml/2 tbsp clear honey

120ml/4fl oz/½ cup bourbon

1 Put the biscuits in a plastic bag and crush them finely with a rolling pin. Tip the crumbs into a bowl and stir in the chopped nuts, cocoa powder and half the icing sugar. Add the honey and bourbon. Stir until the mixture forms a stiff paste. Add a little more bourbon if necessary.

2 Knead and shape the mixture into small balls, place on a plate and chill until firm.

3 Roll the balls in the remaining icing sugar, then chill for 15 minutes and roll again in sugar. Serve in a pretty dish, or pack into a presentation box.

VARIATION
Brandy snaps can be used instead of the biscuits and cognac or brandy instead of the bourbon.

MOCHA TRUFFLES WITH COFFEE LIQUEUR

This melt-in-the-mouth mixture of coffee liqueur and chocolate is irresistible.

MAKES ABOUT 25

175g/6oz dark (bittersweet) chocolate, broken into squares

50g/2oz/¼ cup unsalted (sweet) butter

10ml/2 tsp instant coffee

30ml/2 tbsp double (heavy) cream

225g/8oz/4 cups Madeira or slab cake crumbs

50g/2oz/½ cup finely ground almonds

30ml/2 tbsp Toussaint or other coffee liqueur

cocoa powder (unsweetened), chocolate vermicelli (sprinkles) or finely ground almonds, to coat

1 Put the chocolate, butter and instant coffee in a heatproof bowl. Sit the bowl over a pan of hot water until the chocolate and butter have melted and the coffee has dissolved. (Avoid overheating the chocolate by not letting the water boil or allowing the bowl to touch the water.)

2 Remove from the heat and stir in the cream, cake crumbs, ground almonds and coffee liqueur.

3 Chill the mixture. Shape into small balls, roll in chocolate vermicelli, cocoa powder or ground almonds and put in foil petit-four cases.

VARIATION
Omit the coffee and use cherry brandy instead of the coffee liqueur. For a sweet surprise, hide a maraschino cherry in each truffle.

STEP 1

STEP 3

STEP 2

STEP 3

INDEX